who knew?

Essential Holiday Tips

Secret Savers for a Stress-Free Christmas and Beyond

Bruce Lubin & Jeanne Bossolina-Lubin

© 2012 Castle Point Publishing, LLC

Castle Point Publishing
58 Ninth Street
Hoboken, NJ 07030
www.castlepointpub.com

Cover design by Michele L. Trombley

ISBN: 978-0-9883264-2-2

Printed and bound in the United States of America

2 4 6 8 10 9 7 5 4 3 1

Please visit us online at www.WhoKnewTips.com

TABLE OF CONTENTS

Introduction

No doubt about it, holidays are simultaneously the most fun *and* most stressful times of the year. If you're anything like us, you also relish the quality time, the days off from work, the delicious meals, and, of course, the celebrating! The planning, cleaning, organizing, and hosting can be fun, too, but that's usually where the stress comes in.

Enter: *Who Knew? Essential Holiday Tips.*

This handy guide will walk you through an entire year of holidays, from Valentine's Day to New Year's Eve, plus a chapter on birthdays and parties for any time of year. Jam-packed with tips and creative ideas for hosting celebrations in your home, this book is helpfully organized in chronological order: After reading about some of our favorite birthday and party tips, head to Valentine's Day, then move on to St. Patrick's Day, Easter, Fourth of July, Halloween, Thanksgiving, Christmas, and New Year's!

From tasty food and decorations to activities and post-holiday cleanup, we've got you covered. Not only will your holidays run smoothly, they'll also be remembered by family and friends forever!

Thriftily yours,
Jeanne and Bruce

CHAPTER 1

Fun Tips for Birthdays and Parties

Birthday Photo Collage

We love this creative idea for jazzing up party decor. Collect all the photographs you can find that celebrate your guest of honor—from babyhood, childhood, school yearbooks, vacations, and other memorable events. Then compile them into a large wall collage: Arrange the photos into giant numbers to mark the person's age or year of birth, spell out a name or meaningful word or phrase, or simply form a fun shape.

Candy Cone Centerpiece

What do kids love more than candy? Answer: not much. So this candy centerpiece is always a hit at our boys' birthday parties. You'll need a piece of florist foam in the shape of a cone, plus lots and lots of yummy candy—choose your kids' favorites and also grab a few bags of lollipops. Set the foam cone on top of a tray, plate, or bowl loaded with candy. Insert lollipop sticks into the foam to cover it completely. If you like, make a cardboard or paper number for the guest of honor's age; alternatively, you can use a fun photo. Glue or tape the number to a skewer, then stick it through the top of the cone.

✳ READER'S TIP ✳

For your next kids' party, consider using balloons as "place cards" for each guest (as long as there aren't too many!). Blow up enough balloons for every guest at the party, and use a marker to write a name on each one. Tie the balloons to the chairs around the table, and you've got assigned seats and cute party favors!

—*Sarah Cataldo, Tampa, Florida*

For Bigger Birthday Bashes

Thinking about throwing your child's birthday party in a larger venue? Contact local toddler co-ops and day-care centers to see if you can rent out their space on the weekend—some organizations offer fantastic rates!

Bowling Party in the Backyard!

If your kids love to bowl as much as ours do, this party will be a memorable hit! On flat ground, create a bowling lane with different-colored party streamers. For the pins, collect 10 plastic bottles filled with water, and drop a bit of food coloring in each. Arrange the pins in proper formation at the end of the bowling lane. Use a soccer ball or basketball to as your bowling ball and get your kids ready to score!

✳ CLASSIC TIP ✳

When it comes to piñatas, the spoils go to the bullies, but not if you separate the candies and prizes into Ziploc bags for each guest before stuffing them inside the papier-mâché animal. The kids will still get a rush of excitement when the piñata drops, but the game won't dissolve into an "Are we having fun yet?" moment when they start fighting over Tootsie Rolls and Milky Ways.

For Crystal-Clear Glassware

Do your party glasses look a little murky? To make them sparkle again, pour in a couple tablespoons of lemon juice and then fill the glasses with hot water; leave for three hours or longer, then rinse and wash as usual. Lemons contain light, natural acids that work wonders on glass. You can also try this trick with glass pitchers, decanters, coffee pots, and vases.

Crystal Cleanup

Notice a scratch in your crystal? You can make it disappear in no time with a spot of toothpaste. (Yep, we said toothpaste!) Squeeze a bit of the white, non-gel kind onto a dry cloth, then wipe over the scratch. Rinse it off and dry your crystal—the scratch should be gone! Repeat if necessary.

✳ CLASSIC TIP ✳

To keep meat or cheese hors d'oeuvres moist, cover them first with a damp paper towel, then cover loosely with plastic wrap. Many fillings (as well as bread) dry out very quickly, but with this tip, you can make these simple appetizers first and have them ready on the table when guests arrive.

Sundae Fun

Repurpose a plastic ice cube tray by making it into a killer sundae station. Use the various compartments for nuts, crushed cookies, candy, and other toppings, then serve with ice cream and let the kids make their own sundaes. (Don't be surprised if they dump everything on top.)

✳ CLASSIC TIP ✳

If you're mailing out invitations, stick them in the mailbox on Wednesday, so that they'll arrive on Friday or Saturday. People respond more quickly to mail received on the weekend, and you'll get your headcount finalized sooner!

Get Jiggle with It

We love making Jell-O Jigglers for kids' party snacks— they're easy, sweet, and fun to eat. The best part? Jell-O pieces can take so many different forms! For your next batch, use your child's Duplos or Mega Bloks as molds (just be sure to wash them first!). Kids will love their edible "toys"!

Flat Cookie Fix

Do your cookies come out thin and flat rather than thick and chewy? Sprinkle some flour on the baking sheet after you grease it but before you put the cookie dough down on top of it. The flour will keep your cookies from spreading out, which can be caused by the slickness of the greasy baking sheet.

Crumb-Free Cake Frosting

One of the trickiest things about frosting a cake is making sure that crumbs don't turn your smooth icing into a lump-filled mess. The secret that many pastry chefs use is to dollop spoonfuls of icing a couple of inches apart all over the top of the cake, and simply use a spatula to spread them out.

Maximize Every Morsel

Got a round cake to serve for dessert? Rather than cutting long messy slices, try this carving technique: Cut a ring around the cake to create a smaller cake at the center. Slice the outer ring into rectangular wedges, then slice the inner circle as you would a pizza pie. Serve the icing-heavy wedges to the kids; save the daintier slices for the grown-ups.

Hold Your Cake and Eat It, Too

Little kids usually end up eating cake with their hands anyway, so try this fun dessert treat: Place flat-bottomed ice cream cones in a high-sided baking pan and fill them two-thirds full with cake batter. Bake them at 325°F for 30 minutes, and once they cool you can hold your cake and eat it, too!

On-the-Spot Marshmallow Topping

Need a quick, delicious topping for your party cupcakes? Try this: During the final few minutes of baking time, place one large marshmallow on top of each cupcake. As the cooking continues, the marshmallows will melt into a sweet, sticky frosting—they're done when the tops become lightly browned. Yum!

Easy Mint-Chocolate Frosting

Here's another last-minute cupcake topping idea, this time using tasty chocolate-covered mints. When your cupcakes have baked and cooled, drop a mint on top of each one. Heat the cupcakes in the microwave, one by one, for just a few seconds. Remove and spread the melted mint-chocolate over the top.

If you've ever over-baked a pound cake, you probably know that the fork-doneness test isn't very effective. That's because you typically fork-test the center of a cake. However, the center of a pound cake is always super-moist, even when the baking time is over—it only hardens completely once the cake cools. You'll get an accurate gauge on your pound cake if you test closer to the edge (say, one-third of the way in).

—*Nicole Edmonds-Smith, Trenton, New Jersey*

Cream-Filled Cupcakes

Add a delicious surprise to your birthday cupcakes this year: a creamy center. It's easier than you think! Once your cupcakes are baked and cooled, poke a hole through the top of each one with a straw. Using a pastry bag or a Ziploc bag with a hole cut in the corner, pipe the frosting into the hole that you made with the straw. When you're finishing piping, spread frosting over the tops to cover the hole, or hide it with a chocolate chip or other candy.

Have Cake, Will Travel

If you've already frosted your cake and need to cover it with plastic wrap, first spray the underside of the wrap with nonstick spray. The wrap should remove easily, with no mess!

Keep Beer Sudsy

Serving bottled beer at your party? Consider offering each drinker a matchstick along with the brew. If you place one matchstick over the mouth of the bottle, you'll prevent the beer from going flat.

Cold Drinks the Fun Way

You've decorated your home for your party, so don't stop with your drinks table! Make it festive by filling up balloons with water and freezing them. Place them in a lined basket or decorative bin with beers and sodas for a fun display that also keeps your drinks cool.

CHAPTER 2

Valentine's Day Savers

Sweetheart Stencil

For an ultra-romantic touch on a baked treat, create a sweet heart shape with powdered sugar. Fold a sheet of paper in half, and trace one half of a heart shape along the fold. Cut it out and open the paper heart; there's your stencil. Place it on a piece of toast, a cake, or cookies, sprinkle powdered sugar inside it, then lift—a powdered-sugar heart for your sweetheart!

Lunch Is for Lovers, Too!

For a little less formality on Valentine's Day, consider taking your sweetie out to a romantic lunch or brunch rather than dinner. Not only will you make it more special by sharing it with fewer people (everyone else will probably be making dinner reservations), the lunch menu is usually less expensive.

Put a Little Love in a Jar

Bring some sweetness to your table by placing candy hearts in a vase or Mason jar. Bonus? The candies never grow stale, so you can save this sweet showpiece for next year, too.

✳ CLASSIC TIP ✳

If you're sending flowers this Valentine's Day, skip the national delivery services and websites. Instead, find a flower shop that is local to the recipient and call them directly. Most national services simply charge you a fee, then contact these very same stores themselves.

Balloon Canopy Bed

Celebrate your relationship by making a balloon display above your bed. Get one balloon for each year or month you've been together, and attach a note to each one containing a memory you've shared or a place you've visited as a couple. The colors of the balloons floating above you will create a unique, romantic ambience.

Couples Coupons

Most busy couples don't have time to treat themselves (and each other) to special activities, like massages, breakfasts in bed, and romantic fondue nights. That's why we love giving one another personalized coupons, or IOUs, as gifts. To do this, compile a stack of "coupons" for special activities or freebie chores—one month of laundry, three mowed lawns, one dinner-and-a-movie night—and gift it for a birthday, Valentine's Day, or any holiday. It's creative and fun, and lets your partner choose how he or she wants to be spoiled. Does it get any more romantic than that?

Baking with Heart

Once Christmas is over, snag a bag of tiny candy canes that are on sale and use them for these heart-shaped

cupcake toppers. Flip one cane over and place them together ("hooks" and bottom edges touching). Bake on a nonstick baking sheet at 325°F for 3–5 minutes. Pinch together to seal, then cool and remove with a spatula. They're perfect for decorating cupcakes on Valentine's Day!

✳ CLASSIC TIP ✳

If you don't really have a way with words, steal them from the pros! At Poets.org, you'll not only find tons of classic and contemporary love poems, you can also include one in an e-card to send to loved ones. To make it more romantic, however, try printing out a poem to read aloud on Valentine's Day, or pasting it inside a homemade card.

Leave a Trail of Love Notes

This romantic gesture is perfect for Valentine's Day and the whole rest of the year! Who wouldn't enjoy finding hidden declarations of love all year round? Either purchase a pack of valentines or create your own using pretty paper; on each one, write down something you love about your partner. Then place the notes all over the house, even in unexpected places.

Candy Dots Valentine

Here's an adorable Valentine's Day treat for your child's classmates. And the kids can help make these, too! You'll need a few sheets of candy dots (also known as candy "buttons"), colored construction paper, scissors, scalloped scissors (if you like), and glue. Cut heart shapes out of the candy sheets, then glue each heart to colored construction paper (if it matches the candy color, even better!). For a pretty decorative border, use scalloped scissors to cut a larger heart "frame" out of the construction paper.

Heart-Shaped Cupcakes

You don't need a special tin to make charming, heart-shaped cupcakes or muffins for Valentine's Day. Simply place cupcake liners inside a regular tin, then stick a marble or ball of foil between each liner and the tin. This will create a V-shape for the top of the heart. Pour enough batter to fill the liners only slightly more than halfway. (Don't pour too much, or the heart shapes won't come through!) Bake as directed, and decorate as you like.

CHAPTER 3

Lucky St. Patrick's Day Tips

Shamrock Pepper Stamp

Making St. Patty's Day decorations with the kids? To fashion a stamp in the shape of a shamrock, simply cut off the bottom of a bell pepper—*voilà*! Dip the clover shape in green paint and stamp away!

✳ READER'S TIP ✳

Bring some Irish spirit to the breakfast table by adding a few drops of green food coloring to pancake or waffle batter. Stir the coloring in gradually until you get the shade of green you want, and prepare as usual.

—*Jillian Garvey, Tucson, Arizona*

St. Patty's Free Party Emporium

Yep, we said "free"! For adorable holiday decorations that you can print out at home, check out LivingLocurto. com/2012/03/st-patricks-free-printables. You'll find festive signs, bottle wrappers, drink flags, cake toppers, cupcake wrappers, and more!

Bring a Little Irish Luck to Your Doorstep

Here's another great holiday project for you and the kids: Turn a plain-old flowerpot into an adorable green leprechaun hat. In addition to a clay pot, get some green paint and a paintbrush, a large metal washer (for the buckle), sandpaper to sand down the washer, gold paint, thick black ribbon, and a hot glue gun. Paint the pot green and set it aside to dry. Sand the washer to make it smooth and ready for painting; paint it completely with gold paint. Once both the pot and washer are dry, use your hot glue gun to secure the black ribbon around the center of the pot. Glue the washer—or buckle—on top of the ribbon, and your leprechaun hat pot is ready to grow some shamrocks!

Luck Be a Rainbow Collage

There really *is* a pot of gold at the end of the rainbow!
At the end of this rainbow, at least. You and the kids
can make this simple rainbow collage in a snap—all
you'll need are paper plates, scissors, paints in all six
colors of a rainbow, cotton balls, white glue, and gold
glitter or sparkly paint. Slice a paper plate in half with
your scissors, then paint the arches of a rainbow onto
one half-circle. Dab a few cotton balls in glue and paste
them along the bottom of each arch to form clouds. For
the gold treasure, mix the glitter with a bit of glue to
make a glittery paste, then paint gold coins near one
end of the rainbow.

Corned Beef Cook Test

For lip-smacking, perfectly tender corned beef this St.
Patrick's Day (or any day), give your meat the fork-slip
doneness test: Poke a carving fork into the roast and lift
upward slowly and carefully. The fork should slip out of
the meat cleanly if it's moist and tender.

CHAPTER 4

Egg-cellent Easter Ideas

No-Break Easter Eggs

Before you hard-boil eggs for decorating this year, prevent cracks by first poking a tiny hole in one end of the egg with a pin or needle (make sure it's clean!).

Easy Marbled Easter Eggs

These eggs are even cooler-looking than other marbled eggs. Rather than dyeing just the outer shell, our food coloring seeps into the shells' cracks to create neat spider-web effects. First, hard-boil your eggs as usual.

Once they're cooled, tap each egg on a hard surface to make cracks in the shell—but don't peel! Using a spoon, drip food coloring all over the eggs, and let them dry. Rinse with water and peel the shells. You'll have beautiful marbled eggs that are ready to eat!

✳ CLASSIC TIP ✳

You might think only older kids can dye Easter eggs, but we started our boys off when they were still in diapers. Give your little helpers a plastic container filled with food coloring, water, and a little vinegar. Let them drop the hard-boiled egg in, help them seal it closed, and tell them to gently "shake, shake, shake." Pure magic.

Easter Egg Hunters

If you're hosting an egg hunt for kids of various ages, try color-coding the eggs by age group. Yellow eggs might be hidden in easy-to-find places for the younger kids, while green eggs can be stowed in sneakier spots for the big kids.

Beat-the-Sweets Easter Treat

We like to mix up our Easter snacks so the kids aren't eating *only* sugary sweets. This snack is a little more healthful than the usual candy, plus it's super-cute and Easter-colorful. Pour cheesy Goldfish crackers into a clear plastic pastry bag and tie the opening closed with green ribbon: You've got a carrot! (At least in shape, if not nutritional value.) If you don't have a pastry bag, you can also use the corner of a sandwich bag and some tape.

✳ READER'S TIP ✳

Make Easter dinner even more fun for the kids (and big kids, too!) by putting together these adorable table settings. You'll need orange paper dinner napkins, green plastic utensils, and green pipe cleaners. Fold each napkin in half to form a rectangle. Set a plastic spoon, fork, and knife on a bottom corner of each napkin, then roll the utensils up in the napkin. Wrap a couple of pipe cleaners around the top of each rolled-up napkin, and your carrot table settings will be good enough to eat!

—*Janine Ward-Garrett, Kew Gardens, New York*

Easter Egg Tats

Punch up your Easter eggs this year by applying temporary tattoos in addition to colorful dyes. Your kids will want to put the tats on themselves, too!

Berry Cool Easter Baskets

Here's another creative tip for putting together cute baskets for the kids: Reuse the colorful berry baskets you find at the grocery store! Attach a pipe cleaner on each side of the basket to form a handle, and either tie or glue a small bow to the very top of the handle. Weave colored ribbon through the tiny openings in the basket and secure the ends with glue. Finally, fill it with all sorts of Easter goodies: grass at the bottom, then candy, chocolates, marshmallow Peeps, cookies, and toys!

✳ CLASSIC TIP ✳

Never, ever pay for egg dye! Simply mix ½ cup boiling water with ½ teaspoon white vinegar, and add food coloring until you get a hue you like. For a striped egg even the Easter Bunny would be proud of, wrap tape around the egg before dipping. Once the egg dries, remove the tape, tape over the colored parts, and dip again in a different color. You can also use stickers in the shapes of hearts, stars, and letters.

Egg-Dye Turntable

Egg decorating can turn into a sloppy affair, with various bowls of dye shuffling around your worktable. Make it more efficient by using a lazy Susan to hold your dyes. That way, you can keep everything in one easy-to-maneuver place and avoid messy mishaps.

Remove Dye Stains from Your Skin

Got Easter egg dye on your hands? Remove stains on your skin with this easy solution: Spoon 2 tablespoons salt into a small bowl and gradually mix in vinegar until you have a paste. Scrub your skin with the salt-vinegar paste and stains will disappear in no time!

Savor Your Ham Post-Easter Dinner

Our delicious, succulent ham always goes quickly at Easter. But did you know that you can also save the juice and cook with it later? Just remove the fat and store the juice in small plastic containers or ice cube trays. Use a cube of ham juice to add some flavor to soups, potatoes, and casseroles whenever you want a tasty kick!

CHAPTER 5

Tips for a Fun Fourth and Other Summer Holidays

Independence Day Decorative Stars

For a little added flair at your Fourth of July shindig, set your table with colorful jars adorned with stars! The secret ingredient is Epsom salts. Using white glue, trace a star onto the front of each jar. Dab the still-wet star into a dish of Epsom salts, and set it aside to dry. Then spray paint each jar in a different patriotic color; let dry. When you're ready to party, fill each starred jar with napkins, utensils, straws, and anything else your guests will need at the dinner table.

✳ READER'S TIP ✳

Here's a festive way to incorporate some patriotism into your Independence Day snacks: American flag open sandwiches! Spread cream cheese onto two slices of bread, then smear some red jam on top. Line up banana slices to form the stripes, and add blueberries in the top left corner for the stars. America the beautiful (and delicious!).

—Annie Ortiz, Oakland, California

Land of the Free, Home of the Boozy

Do you have some patriotic tipplers joining you for the Fourth? Mix up this tasty summertime cocktail that is sure to whet their whistles: Combine 1 ounce vodka, 1 ounce strawberry schnapps, and 3 ounces club soda. Then top it off with blueberries.

Fourth Decor

Celebrate in festive style by making some holiday-themed decorations! If you can find a "4" birthday candle or house number, display it inside a large glass vase. Then fill the vase with red, white, and blue candies, and slip miniature American flags inside.

Protect Little Hands from Sparkler Sparks!

Kids and grownups alike love Fourth of July fireworks—especially low-cost, safe-to-handle ones, like sparklers. The flying sparks are both exciting *and* a little dangerous! To protect yourselves from getting burned by sparklers, before lighting them, poke the unlit end through the inside of a plastic drinking cup. The burning end should stick out through the bottom of the cup, while your hand is safely contained inside holding the handle.

Bedeck Your Deck

Bring a little patriotism to the outside of your home by making bunting for your porch rail. All you'll need is an appropriate yardage of USA-themed fabric and some colored yarn to tie it up. Tie one end of fabric to the end of your rail. Then, about every two feet, bunch the fabric and tie it to the rail with the yarn.

You're hosting a backyard barbecue that's turned into an evening affair. Unfortunately, your outdoor accent lights aren't bright enough, but you don't want to have to turn on the glaring light by your door. Instead, fold pieces of aluminum foil in half (shiny side out) and wrap like a bowl around the bottom of the light, then attach with a few pieces of electrical tape. The foil will reflect the light in a nice, shimmering pattern.

Party Bees Not Allowed!

If you can't beat 'em, join 'em (kind of). At your next picnic party give stinging party crashers like bees and wasps a treat of their own—a few cans of open beer around the perimeter of your yard. They'll go for the beer and stay away from your guests. You can also try using sugar-covered grapefruit halves.

All-Natural Fly Repellent

Heading to a picnic and hate the thought of all the flies that will be dive-bombing your al fresco feast? Keep them away with an easy addition to your picnic basket. Just poke some whole cloves into several lemon wedges, then place them around the edges of your picnic blanket. The flies can't stand the scent and will stay away.

Barricade Your Grub from Bugs

Here's an easy and safe way to defend your picnic or barbecue from insect invasions. Smear lots of petroleum jelly onto the legs of your table—from the very bottom to about two inches up. Little bug legs are no match for the gummy, sticky barricade.

✳ CLASSIC TIP ✳

Include some sprigs of fresh mint in your picnic basket when eating al fresco. Bees and wasps don't like mint, so add some to your plate to keep it stinger-free.

The No-Stick Grilling Trick

Prevent a sticky grill grate by lightly coating your food with oil before it touches the grill: Place veggies or meat in a zip-tight plastic bag. Add a small amount of olive oil to the bag, seal it up, and rub the oil onto the surface of the food through the plastic. The light oil rub will ensure that your food is juicy and ultra-tasty, and it won't stick to your grill!

Sugar Does It

Can't get the charcoal going, and don't have any lighter fluid? Try using sugar. Once sugar is exposed to a flame, it decomposes rapidly and releases a fire-friendly chemical that can help ignite that stubborn charcoal. Simply apply a light dusting of sugar to the coals before you light them.

Searing Savvy

For a deliciously crisp and juicy piece of seared meat, make sure your grill reaches the optimum temperature— ultra hot. Preheat it for 10 minutes, then wait until a gray ash develops over the coals. If you're using a gas grill, you can find the optimal preheating times in the manual.

✳ READER'S TIP ✳

Fish on the grill is a family favorite in our house—not only is it delicious, it's also super-nutritious, so we love serving it as often as possible over the summer. The tricky part? Fish tends to stick to the hot grill grates, leaving you with grilled fish scraps rather than plump fillets. For extra lubrication, try coating the fish in mayonnaise instead of oil—the thicker texture makes it harder for the flesh to grip the metal. Plus, mayo adds a new layer of yummy seasoning.

—*Samantha Paul, Chevy Chase, Maryland*

For Succulent Grilled Corn

There's nothing more delicious than perfectly juicy corn on the cob straight off the grill. To keep the corn from drying out during cooking, we leave the husks intact the entire time—this keeps the moisture in, ensuring that our corn is steamed and juicy. First, stick the cobs in a bowl or sink filled with cold water; let them soak for 15 minutes. Then place them on the grill, still unshucked. Grill until tender, turning occasionally, about 20 minutes. When you're ready to dig in, pull the husks and silks back to the ends of the cob and use them as handles.

Just Say "No" to Lighter Fluid

When the coals start to die down on your grill, don't squirt them with more lighter fluid, which not only costs money, but can also leave your food tasting bad (not to mention burn the hair off your arm). Instead, blow a hair dryer on the base of the coals. The hair dryer acts as a pair of bellows, and your fire will be going again in no time.

✳ CLASSIC TIP ✳

If you're grilling a steak on a closed barbecue, here's a neat trick to impress your friends. Open a can of beer and place it on the hottest part of the grill. It will boil and keep the meat moist, while adding flavor, too.

Great Grill Cleaner

Your barbecue chicken was a hit, but your grill is a mess. What to do? Poke half an onion on your grill fork, dip in vegetable oil, and scrub it over the hot grates. The onion's enzymes will break down grime, and the oil will help soften the grilled-on yunk.

Crafty Homemade Cooler

Heading to the beach or a picnic without a cooler? Keep your food cold with this trick: Store your food containers in the refrigerator for a few hours so they're sufficiently chilled before you need them. Use a few sheets of newspaper to line the inside of a picnic basket or tote bag—the paper will trap in the cold and keep out the heat. Place the chilled containers into your lined bag or basket, layering more sheets of newspaper on top of each container.

For a Crisp Salad on Warm Days

Nobody at the barbecue wants to eat a wilted salad, but the warm seasonal temps make it tough to keep the lettuce crisp. To prevent it from wilting, stick a metal soup pot in the freezer for one hour—the ice-cold metal will be a perfect makeshift cooler for your veggies. Store and serve your tossed salad in the chilled pot. It should stay fresh for two hours!

Frugal Boozing

No summertime gathering is complete without family, friends, fun, and lots of refreshing good-time beverages. (Translation: beer.) Sales on beer and wine usually start on the Sunday or Wednesday before a holiday, so wait until then to stock up. Or, check out SaveOnBrew.com, a site that locates beer sales in your neighborhood. Just enter your zip code and, voilà, up-to-the-minute discounts!

✳ CLASSIC TIP ✳

The best way to chill beer or soda rapidly is to fill a cooler with layers of water, ice, and salt, then plunge the beverages inside. In about 20 minutes or less, the beer will be ice cold! Even if the ice water is warmer than your freezer, it absorbs the warmth from the bottles or cans more rapidly and more efficiently than the cold air of the freezer does. Just remember that premium lagers should be served between 42°F and 48°F and ales between 44°F and 52°F, so don't let them get too cold.

Picnic Pointer

Keep your picnic tablecloth in place on windy days by using clothespins: Hot glue one clothespin underneath each corner of the table. Clip the ends of the

tablecloth into the pins, and those wind gusts will be no match for your party!

Your Go-To Picnic Preservative: Mayo

Planning for a picnic? It may surprise you to learn you should use more mayonnaise! In addition to being delicious, the silky condiment also has bacteria-fighting acids, which help your food stay fresh longer in the sun. Add more of it to side dishes like potato salad, chicken salad, and pasta salad for optimum food-poisoning protection.

Prevent Soggy Slaw

Coleslaw is one of our summertime faves, but the shred-ded cabbage salad always tends to turn soggy and limp before we've made it to a second helping. Luckily, we've found a prep tip that helps keep cabbage crunchy for longer: Place a head of cabbage in a large bowl or pot, fill it with ice-cold water, then add 1 tablespoon salt for every two quarts water. Let soak for 10 minutes. The salt absorbs water, helping the cabbage stay hydrated and crisp even once it's shredded and mixed into a salad.

Munchable Fresh-Cut Veggies

If you'll have crudités at your outdoor party, keep those cut veggies fresh and crunchy by storing them properly: Place damp paper towels over the vegetables and wrap everything in plastic wrap. Stick the wrapped veggies in the fridge until it's time to serve. Carrots, broccoli, and peppers will stay bright and crisp for 12 hours.

Weekend Roadtrip Tip

Popular travel weekends usually mean hiked-up gas prices. Think ahead this year and refill your tank a few days before any big holiday escapes—you'll avoid the higher prices and your car will be road-ready before the traffic hits (hopefully!).

CHAPTER 6

Spook-tacular Halloween Hints

Glowing Ghost Eyes

Scaring trick-or-treaters is a huge part of the fun at our house. This super-simple outdoor prop is a doozy! Trace two eyes onto a cardboard toilet paper tube, and cut them out. Place glow sticks inside the tube, and set your ghostly eyes in a sneaky-but-visible spot near your doorstep—in a bush or potted plant beside the front door.

Adding stretchy cobwebs to the doorjambs and corners of your home is a great way to give Halloween flair to the entire house. Instead of buying the ones packaged as spider webs, though, simply go to a craft store and buy a bag of fiberfill. It's the exact same stuff, and a 16-ounce bag of fiberfill is less than half the cost. You can also usually find inexpensive bags of plastic spider rings at party supply or superstores—add them to the webs and on tables around your house for more atmosphere, and encourage your guests to take them home!

Make Way for House Ghosts

Need some creepy Halloween decorations on the cheap? Of course you do! Here's a super-easy tip for making floating ghosts for the outside of your home: Open a white plastic garbage bag and stuff a balled-up newspaper into the very bottom. Tighten the bag around the ball and tie it closed with a rubber band—this is the ghost's head and neck. Use a black Sharpie to draw a ghoulish face, then hang it in your front yard or near the doorstep to scare trick-or-treating guests.

The Early Ghoul Catches the Worm

Just like Christmas, you'll find the best Halloween deals way before the day actually rolls around. But why not start even earlier? During the week after Halloween, most related merchandise is deeply discounted—often 75 percent off! Shopping for costumes and decorations almost a year in advance might sound silly, but you'll save lots of cash, time, and stress prepping for next year.

Safe Storage for Vinyl Decals

Vinyl stickies look great on windows, doors, and other surfaces around the house. But when you remove them, they tend to wrinkle and stick to themselves, making them unusable for future Halloweens. Prevent damage to your decals by laying them flat on a sheet of aluminum foil; then top them with another sheet of foil and fold the edges over to protect them. Store the decals flat with your other Halloween decorations, and they'll be in great shape for next year.

Pumpkin Pointer

Got cookie cutters on hand? Use them to make cool shapes in your jack-o'-lantern! Hold the cutter against the pumpkin's shell, and use a rubber mallet to hit it softly until it penetrates—the cutter should enter at least halfway through the shell. Pull out the cutter, then trace the shape with a small serrated knife to remove the image from the shell.

✳ CLASSIC TIP ✳

Keep your jack-o'-lantern from withering into looking like an old man! Spray the inside of the hollowed-out pumpkin with an antiseptic spray, which slows down the bacterial growth and increases the time it takes for the pumpkin to deteriorate. Just make sure no one eats a pumpkin that has been sprayed! You can also try using WD-40 spray instead.

Pumpkin Goop Scooper

When you're carving your pumpkin this fall, rather than using a spoon or your bare hands to scoop out the goopy insides, try an ice cream scooper instead! Less labor, less sticky mess, and more time for the actual carving.

The Ever-Glowing Pumpkin

A candle looks eerily beautiful when burning inside a carved pumpkin, but electric lights last longer and burn even more brightly. To give your pumpkin a long-lasting glow, curl up a string of Christmas lights, stick them in a clear plastic bag, and place the bag inside the pumpkin. Carve a small hole in the back of your pumpkin to plug the lights into an electrical outlet.

Estimate Your Trick-or-Treater Turnout

If you've ever stood in the Halloween candy aisle asking yourself, "How many bags should I buy?" you'll love this tip. As you refill your candy bowl this Halloween, keep track of how many empty bags you've got at the end of the night. Record this number somewhere safe, such as on your computer or smartphone calendar. (You can even set a pop-up reminder for next year's Halloween.) That way, you'll know approximately how much candy to buy ahead of time!

Bloody Good Gore-fest

Nothing says Halloween like chainsaw-inflicted gashes and lots of zombie fluids. Cook up your own fake blood this year by mixing cornstarch, red and blue food dye, and a little milk. Use a small paintbrush to work your bloody magic on faces, necks, limbs, and clothing (warning: it may stain!).

Scare Up Some Face Paint

Skip the store-bought face paint this year (along with those yucky chemicals) and make your own nontoxic paints! All you'll need are a few common household items and food coloring: Combine 5 tablespoons corn-starch, 2 tablespoons shortening, 1 tablespoon flour, and a drop of petroleum jelly. Split this mixture into several different containers and add the food dyes as you need them.

Face Paint Remover

Face paint is an important part of our kids' Halloween fun. But getting it off easily can be a problem. One trick that's worked for us is olive oil: Simply rub it onto the skin with a dry cloth, then wipe off with a wet cloth.

Peanut Allergy Prevention

Are there any peanut allergies in your house? They can really put a damper on a child's trick-or-treating fun. To prevent any mishaps and still let your kids enjoy their Halloween outing, have some safe, peanut-free candy at home waiting for them. When your witches and ghouls return from their neighborhood prowl, go through their hauls with them and swap the questionable candies with your nut-free stash.

Trick or Treasure

Instead of candy this year, hand out cool party favors to all your trick-or-treaters. They might not be as conventional as the usual sweet treats, but they're still really fun and can save you some cash. Hit the dollar store and pick up packages of stickers, temporary tattoos, finger puppets, or other amusing little toys.

✳ CLASSIC TIP ✳

Finding dry ice to put at the bottom of the punch bowl can be a bit difficult, so to make your punch seem haunted quickly and easily, freeze grapes to use as ice cubes. Once they're frozen, peel off the skin and they'll look like creepy eyeballs.

Spooky Skeleton Snacks

Here's a Halloween take on a favorite seasonal snack: Bake gingerbread cookies in the shape of humans or animals, then ice them as skeletons.

Frankenstein Fingers

These string-cheese snacks are healthy *and* totally creepy. Serve them at a Halloween party or sneak them inside your kids' lunches for a little scare. First, make the knuckles by cutting slits in the string cheese where the knuckles should be. Cut small rectangles out of a green pepper and press them into the tips of the cheese strips to form the monster's fingernails. If needed, add a little cream cheese as an adhesive to keep the nails in place.

Save on Last-Minute Candy Runs

If Halloween is coming up and you still haven't picked up your candy, don't worry! (There will *never* be a candy shortage in America.) The timing might be just right for discounts: Wait until the day before for eleventh-hour flash sales.

Gross-Out Halloween Drinks

Need more spooky treats? Mix up these colorful drinks for the kids. They might look toxic, but they're totally safe—though packed with sugar! Combine one part Mountain Dew and one part blue Kool-Aid to make a Blue Ghost Punch. Or mix a bit of green food coloring into lemonade for a Toxic Tart.

✳ READER'S TIP ✳

For a yummy gross-out snack, prepare a bright-green gelatin mold with gummy worms squirming around in the mix. Just wait until the mold sets a bit, place the gummy worms inside, and stick back in the fridge. Serve while the gelatin is still a little goopy, to best resemble gooey slime.

—*Marianna Riolo, Cozad, Nebraska*

Hobgoblin Punch

Put a little fright into your Halloween party with this clever punch-bowl gag. Pour green Kool-Aid into a latex or rubber glove, tie it closed, then place it in your freezer. When frozen, cut off the glove and place the "goblin hand" in your punch bowl!

CHAPTER 7

Thanksgiving Dinner and Beyond

Festive Fall Decoration

We love this festive-for-fall decoration: Cut a slice off the side of an apple so it lies flat on a saucer or candle-holder. Then cut a hole out of the top, and you have an instant votive or tea-light holder! Coat the hole with some lemon juice to keep it from turning brown.

Post-Halloween Pumpkin Project

With this project, kids can enjoy pumpkin crafts all season long! Get a few small pumpkins—one for each child—and plan a leaf-collecting trip to the park or simply your backyard. Let the leaves dry completely, then use craft glue to paste them all over the pumpkins.

✳ CLASSIC TIP ✳

Give hyper kids something to do *and* decorate your table at the same time this Thanksgiving by sending them out into the yard to find the last remaining yellow, red, and orange leaves. Make sure they're not visibly dirty, then arrange them along the middle of the table in lieu of a runner. We love this activity because it's good for kids of any age, and the older ones can help the younger ones.

Reuse Corn Decor

Are your colorful corncobs missing lots of kernels already? Switch it up! Instead of hanging them on the wall, scrape off the rest of the kernels and pour them into a pretty candleholder, small vase, or Mason jar.

Turkey Day Stains Be Gone!

Prepping for Thanksgiving dinner can be an enormously stressful task—and that's not even counting clean-up time. Here's a great preventative measure we've picked up over the years that helps with our post-meal cleaning: Spray starch your tablecloth a day or two before T-Day, and let it dry for at least a full day. Drips and spills will be no match for your stain-guarded table!

Save a Soupy Stuffing

Without question one of the main attractions at our Thanksgiving table, stuffing is hearty, creamy, and comforting—perfect for this family-centric holiday. However, we've had our share of stuffing mishaps; sometimes it's too goopy and wet to eat. To bring soupy stuffing back to life, first spread it onto a baking sheet. Layer cubes of stale bread or unseasoned croutons on top of the stuffing. Pop it back into the oven for about 15 minutes at 375°; when finished, stir it all together and spoon into a serving dish. The bread will sop up excess liquid, leaving your stuffing in its intended scrumptious form.

Turn Down the Smell, Turn-ip the Taste!

Turnips tend to stink up the house whenever we cook them. To tone down the odor, we add 1 teaspoon sugar to the pot while they're cooking—less odor, more taste!

✳ CLASSIC TIP ✳

This simple trick offers peace of mind when several folding tables are placed together to form a bigger table. To create stability, use cleaned-out coffee cans as holders for adjoining legs from different tables, and rest assured that your grandmother's hand-blown glass punch bowl is safe.

Quick Turkey Fix

Did the star of your Thanksgiving dinner come out too dry? Don't panic! You can re-hydrate your meat with an easy braise: Slice up the turkey and stick it in a baking dish. Fill the dish halfway with chicken stock, top with foil, and place it back in the oven for 10 minutes at 350°. The turkey will be juicy and delicious.

Cleaner Carving

If you've just made a super-juicy turkey, you can congratulate yourself as a cook. But what to do about all of the juices making a mess of your counter as you carve it? Place your cutting board inside a rimmed baking sheet before you cut, and you'll not only have an easy clean-up, you'll also have rich drippings you can use in gravy or broth.

Great Gravy

Of all the delicious food on Thanksgiving, our favorite is the gravy! Give yours a bold, delicious boost with our secret family ingredient: apple cider vinegar. Just mix in a spoonful when you're done with the gravy, and the vinegar will give it a fruity, tangy taste.

Warming Bread Basket

You can keep rolls and biscuits warmer for longer by first lining your basket or bowl with aluminum foil. Cover it with a paper towel or napkin, then place your bread inside.

Custom-Bake Your Biscuits

Biscuits generally come in two delicious varieties: Soft and fluffy or crusty and flaky. If you prefer soft and crumbly, place them next to one another on the baking sheet so they touch. For crusty biscuits, arrange them so there's space between. Do you like your biscuits browned a bit? Spritz them with butter-flavored cooking oil before baking.

CHAPTER 8

Christmas and Holiday Season Tips

Advent Activity Calendar

For a new twist on the usual Advent countdown, make this year's calendar a family to-do list—full of fun activities for you and your kids. Print each day's item onto a small card or sheet of paper, then compile them all into a 25-day calendar. Activities can be anything you'll enjoy doing together: Watch a holiday movie, decorate the tree, make gingerbread cookies, go sledding, drink hot cocoa, or read a Christmas story.

Count down the days till Christmas with this fun family activity: Pull together all of your holiday-themed books and wrap them as individual gifts. Let your children open one gift per night, and read the book together; save "The Night Before Christmas" for the 24th. The pre-holiday festivities might keep your kids satiated enough to lay off the presents under the tree until Christmas!

Invent Your Own Advent Calendar

Let the Christmas countdown begin! Our kids love making their own Advent calendars in anticipation of their number-one favorite holiday of the year. The best part? The "calendar" can be made from anything as long as there are 25 ways to mark off the days until December 25. Here's an easy version to help kick your holiday season into gear: Fasten a clothesline or strand of ribbon to a wall, and attach 25 clothespins. Pin 25 little containers or bags to the clothesline—try small envelopes, cloth sacks, or mini stockings—then slip a little present inside each one. Your kids open one tiny gift per day as yuletide festivities get nearer and nearer.

Snowy Showpieces

Bring some wintry flair indoors by using artificial snow in your table decorations: Sprinkle it onto table displays, around centerpieces, or along a mantel lined with ornaments.

Gift Wrap Your Pillows

Tie shiny Christmas-colored ribbon around your living room throw pillows—try red, green, white, silver, or gold. You can wrap it around the pillow twice, like you would wrap a gift, and tie a big festive bow on the front.

DIY Stocking Alternatives

Shake up your Christmas mantel this year by making stockings out of unusual objects—not only will they be memorable, they are also super-fun to make! Anything from coffee cans to popcorn tins to potato chip tubes will do the trick: Drill or cut a hole near the top of the can, paint the outside a favorite color, and decorate as you like (with paint, candy canes, stickers, or ribbons, for example). Thread a strand of ribbon through the hole and tie a knot to create a loop for hanging.

Christmas-ize Your Bathroom

When you're decorating the house for the holidays, don't forget the bathroom! Punch up the holiday spirit in the loo with holiday-colored bath towels: Gather three different sizes of towels (in three different colors, if possible), and stack them in size order. Tie colored ribbon around the towels to resemble a wrapped gift, and set them on a counter or behind the toilet bowl.

Wrapping Paper Wall Art

Got lots of Christmas paper left over from gift-wrapping? Reuse it as festive wall art! Cut the paper to fit hanging picture frames, then mount on your wall.

Christmas Tree Fresh Test

Opting for a beautiful live tree this year? If you're getting a pre-cut tree, make sure you test its freshness before you buy it—you never know how long it's been sitting in the lot exposed to the elements. Try these quick tests to find the freshest tree possible. The Branch Test: Grab a branch firmly between your fingers and gently pull it toward you, then let it go. If lots of needles shake off the tree, it's not fresh enough; if only a few needles fall, the tree is probably still in decent shape. The Fragrance Test: Snap a needle in your fingers and give it good whiff—the needle should be moist and deliciously pine-scented. If you don't get a pungent dose of pine, the tree is likely drying out.

✳ CLASSIC TIP ✳

We've been known to keep our Christmas tree up until well into January, and with this little trick, you can enjoy the holidays a little longer too. Add a small amount of sugar or Pine-Sol to the water to extend the life of your tree.

Humidifier for a Healthy Tree

The heating system in your home can dry out your tree, dulling its color and piney fresh scent. To give your tree a healthy boost of moisture, place a humidifier in the room to counteract the drying heat—it'll stay fresh, and you can soak up the holiday spirit as long as possible.

First Feeding for the Tree

Just got your tree up? Great job! Next up: The first feeding. Water your tree with hot water—the temp should be around 80 degrees—then add 2 ounces antibacterial mouthwash. Hot water helps the tree start absorbing water efficiently, and the mouthwash keeps bacteria and mold at bay.

Keep Your Tree Luscious with LED Lights

If it's time for new tree lights this year, choose mini LED lights over the traditional kind. Not only do they save energy (and cut the cost of electricity), they're also not as hot, preventing your tree from drying out quickly.

When you take down your Christmas lights, always wrap the strands around the outside of a cardboard tube (try the tube from a roll of paper towels) and secure with masking tape. They'll be easy to unwind next year, and you'll never have another nightmarish day of untangling all the lights while the kids wait to decorate the tree.

Baby-Proofing Your Tree

If your baby is mobile and curious, as those little ones tend to be, be sure to keep the kid and your Christmas tree safe from tiny roaming hands. Use wire to secure the tree to the wall, ceiling, or any nearby railing or banister. And pick up some large bells from a craft store to add to your tree decorations—any pulling or grabbing will shake the bells, alerting you to baby monkey business.

Sap Spill Solution

A real Christmas tree adds a deliciously fragrant touch to holiday festivities. Unfortunately, it can also be messy. To combat sap stains on carpets, pour rubbing alcohol onto a cloth and pat it over the sappy spots. The alcohol will de-stick the sap; then wipe it away with a clean cloth.

Pet-Proof Your Tree

Does your doggie like to lap up the water intended for your Christmas tree? This can be dangerous, thanks to the chemicals lingering in the tree stand. To prevent pets from sneakily re-hydrating at the Christmas tree, wrap the water container in aluminum foil until it reaches several inches up the trunk of your tree. Place your tree skirt over the foil so it isn't visible. When it's time for a refill, simply remove the foil at the top, pour in fresh water, then cover again.

✴ CLASSIC TIP ✴

Don't waste your money on an expensive tree skirt this Christmas. Instead, look for a small, round tablecloth from a department store—they usually have a big selection and they're inexpensive, too. Cut a round opening in the center for the tree stand, and a straight line to one edge. Place the opening in the back of the tree and you're done.

Christmas Cat-astrophe

Cat lovers, beware! When it's time to trim the tree, never use tinsel if you have a pet kitty. Cats love to play with tinsel and eat it, and it can be deadly if it gets stuck in their digestive system.

Make Your Home a Winter Wonderland

Got any spare cupcake liners on hand? Use them to make pretty paper snowflakes for your living room decorations: Set the liners on a flat surface and press to flatten them. Fold each liner in half, and fold in half again. Using scissors, cut shapes into the folds to create your snowflakes. String them all onto one piece of ribbon or yarn to form a garland, or hang them around the room individually for a beautiful snowy scene.

Glassware Decor

Vases, candlesticks, Mason jars, and bowls can all be turned into elegant Christmas baubles. Gather them into one display area and place ornaments, candles, buttons, or ribbons inside them. Or, bring a little bit of winter indoors by filling them with pinecones, twigs, cranberries, or even fake snow.

Give Lamps a Festive Lift

Brighten up your lighting with holiday spirit by securing a red, green, white, or silver ribbon around the circumference of a lampshade.

Sass Up the Staircase

Do you have a beautiful staircase banister you'd like to show off during the holidays? Take full advantage by wrapping garlands around it and hanging poinsettias along the steps. Consider weaving an elegant ribbon or sparkling string lights around the banister for added effect.

How 'Bout Them Apples?

If you ever get one of those plastic containers apples sometimes come in, make sure to save it for your Christmastime storage. It's the perfect holder for holiday ornaments, especially the classic glass orbs.

What to Do with Dusty Decor

Save your family from the dust-inflicted sneezies by airing out your stored holiday decorations before you put them up. If your ornaments or stockings are dusty, quickly clean them by pointing a blow-dryer at them on cool, with a trash bin placed strategically behind them to catch the dust.

✴ CLASSIC TIP ✴

We love the look of pine wreaths and garlands, but hate it when needles get all over the floor. To keep the needles from falling, spritz your holiday greenery with hair spray right after you purchase it. The hair spray will keep the needles moist and where they belong.

Easy-Peasy Pipe Cleaner Ornaments

Need last-minute (and cheap) Christmas tree ornaments? If you have holiday cookie cutters and pipe cleaners on hand, you'll be set in no time. Shape a pipe cleaner around the perimeter of a cookie cutter, making sure you get every corner and bend. When your pipe cleaner shape is complete, twist the ends together to close it up. If your wire is long enough, make a loop at the top for hanging; if not, attach a small loop with another piece of pipe cleaner. For a decorative touch, wrap the pipe cleaner ornament with a thin strip of festive fabric, winding the material around the piping to cover it completely and then knotting it once you've wrapped the entire shape.

Christmas Window Paint

The kids will have fun with this one: Decorate your windows with Christmas greetings and drawings using toothpaste! Not only will the bright-white markings look beautiful from the outside, but once the holiday is over, the toothpaste will also serve as a fantastic window cleaner.

Vacuuming up your Christmas tree's fallen pine needles can end up quickly clogging your vacuum. But (naturally) we have a solution! Cut the leg off of some old pantyhose and slip the toe over the end of the vacuum hose; fasten with a rubber band if necessary. The needles will get caught in the mesh of the nylon, keeping them out of your vacuum entirely. You can even add the loose needles to glasses or jars to make decorations!

—Judy Miller, Wheat Ridge, CO

Over-the-Door Wreath Hanger

Here's an easy way to hang a wreath on your door: Grab one self-adhesive wall hook—the 3M brand is perfect—and hang it upside down on the reverse side of your door. Loop the wreath's hanging ribbon around the hook on the opposite side of the door, then pull it over the top for an over-the-door setup. The wreath should hang securely on the front.

Santa's Recycling System

We love this "toy recycling" idea so much that it's become a favorite tradition in our home. When the kids make their wish lists, they should also decide which old

toys they'd like to give back to Santa for Christmastime recycling—Santa and his elves refurbish the old toys so he can give them to less fortunate children. If your kids are older, bring the toys to the Goodwill or Salvation Army together. Not only does this help de-clutter the house, it also inspires heartwarming Christmas spirit in little kids and big ones alike.

Stop Christmas Day Chaos Before It Starts

Here's an easy way for your kids to tell which presents belong to whom on Christmas morning: Wrap each child's gifts with his or her own wrapping paper. This is especially helpful if your children aren't able to read gift tags yet. It's also a great way to keep the suspense until Christmas Day if you don't tell the kids which wrapping paper denotes whose gifts!

✳ CLASSIC TIP ✳

Use pages from the past year's calendar (photo-side up, obviously) to wrap smaller gifts—two taped together are great for books or DVD sets at Christmastime.

Price Tag De-Sticker

Need to remove those pesky price tag stickers on your Christmas presents? Easy! Try hand sanitizer: The alcohol in the sanitizer works to de-stick the adhesive in the sticker glue. Just rub a bit into the spot and let it sit for a couple minutes, then use a coin to scrape it off.

Gift Wrap Wrapper

Don't let your wrapping paper get ripped or creased before it even makes it onto the present! Cut a lengthwise slit in an empty wrapping paper tube, and wrap it around the roll of paper you'd like to protect. You can leave the very end of the paper sticking out of the cardboard wrapper to create a dispenser.

De-Wrinkle Your Decorations

Planning to package your gifts with bows and ribbons from last year? If they're smashed and wrinkled, don't toss them out! Instead, stick them in the dryer on low heat along with a dampened cloth and run it for two minutes. The heat plus the moisture from the cloth will plump them back to life.

✳ READER'S TIP ✳

Our holiday meals are always decadent and delicious—and also sometimes pretty messy. If someone at your table gets a grease stain during dinner, use cornstarch to absorb the oil. With your fingers, rub a bit onto the stain and let it sit for a few minutes; then wipe it off. Do this as many times as it takes to remove the oil. Finally, pour some dish soap onto the area and wash in hot water.

—*Emily Walsh-Davies, Sarasota, Florida*

Illuminated Place Settings

Light up your table for the holidays with these clever place settings. Purchase a bunch of small votive candle-holders—one for each dinner guest. Write the name of each guest on a slip of paper, then attach the name tags to the candleholders using clear tape. Another fun idea? Print out color photos of your guests to match the size of the candleholders, then use those in lieu of name tags. Either way, they'll be beautifully illuminated by the candles behind them!

Keep Cookies Crisp

Once your cookies are baked, cooled, and ready to be stored in their container, use this tip to ensure they stay crisp and delicious. Place a wad of crumpled-up tissue paper at the very bottom of your container, then fill with cookies and close the lid.

North Pole's Official Letterhead

Santa is *such* an important person, of course he deserves his own stationery! Leave notes for the little ones on Santa's official letterhead, which is available as a free download here: DesignEditor.typepad.com/files/desantastationery.pdf. Or use this charming stationery to send your own (Santa-approved!) Christmas greetings.

Help Cookie Dough Hold Its Shape

With a family as large and busy as ours, we prefer to make big batches of cookie dough ahead of time: We shape the dough into an easy-to-slice rolls and pop them in the freezer until we're ready to do the actual baking. The only problem? The underside of the dough ends up

flattened against the bottom of the freezer. To prevent this, we use paper-towel tubes to hold the rolls of dough and keep them round for cookie-shaped slices. First, wrap the dough in plastic wrap. Make a long cut down the length of a cardboard tube, and place the dough log inside. The dough will keep its tube shape, ensuring that your Christmas cookies are picture perfect!

Luscious Latkes

Making latkes for a Hanukkah dinner? For the best consistency, stick to high-starch potatoes: Yukon gold is the best choice for a richer batch, but standard baking potatoes yield delicious latkes, too. However, you'll want to avoid the waxier red bliss variety, which tend to turn out sticky.

The Starchy Secret to Great Latkes

Want the magic ingredient for the tastiest latkes? Potato starch. Here's how: Shred your potatoes into a bowl of cold water, remove them to another bowl using a strainer, and keep the liquids that remain behind. Wait about 10 minutes for the liquids to separate—the water will rise to the top and leave the chalky-looking potato starch at the bottom. Pour out the water, taking care to save the starch at the bottom of the bowl. Scoop this starch back in with the potatoes.

Make-Ahead Potato Latkes

If you don't have time to prepare latkes on the day of your dinner, you can make them ahead of time and stick them in the freezer. When you're ready to serve, pop them in the oven for 10 minutes at 350°F.

✳ CLASSIC TIP ✳

When it's time to bring down the tree and lights, take great care with the more delicate ornaments. For extra safety, slip them into old socks or nylons, then place them in disposable plastic cups before storing. Old egg cartons are another ultra-safe (and eco-friendly) way to store bulbs and glass trinkets.

Eco-Friendly Tree Disposal

When Christmas is over and you're finally ready to admit it, consider recycling your tree rather than tossing it in the trash. Visit Search.Earth911.com to find recycling centers in your area—they'll shred your trees into reusable mulch, compost, and wood chips, and many offer drop-off and pick-up options.

For Perfect Mulled Wine

One of our no-fail holiday party potables is a sweet-and-spicy mulled wine. Here's an easy trick we've picked up that helps keep our cloves in the pot (and out of our guests' mouths!): Press all cloves into the citrus rinds, such as oranges and lemons. They'll simmer and spice up the pot, and when you ladle the yummy wine into cups, the cloves will stay lodged in the peels.

CHAPTER 9

A New Year's Eve to Remember

Balloon-Popping Countdown

We love shaking up our New Year's parties by incorporating some creative spirit into the mix. Here's a great idea to keep things exciting: On separate slips of paper, write down one activity per hour of the party—for example "Dance, dance, dance!" or "Karaoke time!" Insert each note into a balloon, then blow it up! Write a time on the outside of each balloon, and when that hour arrives during the party, pop the balloon and begin the designated activity. The balloon-popping countdown to midnight and the spontaneity of the party will be super-fun for everyone.

Here's an original idea for a cheap New Year's Eve decoration: gather all the devices you use to tell time—stopwatches, alarm clocks, calendars, pocket planners, even the little hourglasses from board games—and place them on a tray next to the champagne bowl. Tell all your guests to set their alarms for midnight and do the same with the items you've collected.

Bubble Wrap Bop Till You Drop

For a kick-butt kids' party, collect sheets of bubble wrap and lay them on the floor before the clock strikes midnight. Let the kids celebrate the countdown by jumping, dancing, and stomping on the bubbles for a poppin' good time!

Get Silly

Having a New Year's party? Put your child's inexplicable Silly Bandz obsession to good use! These rubber bands in fun shapes are perfect for putting around the stems of wine glasses so your guests can tell whose glass is whose.

If store-bought noisemakers aren't raucous enough for your party, make your own party horns for some serious New Year's hootin'. A cardboard paper towel tube or wax paper roll will do the trick—use whichever you have on hand. Place a piece of wax paper over one end of the tube, and secure it in place with a rubber band or tape. If you like, make your horn extra-festive by covering it in wrapping paper. Use scissors or a knife to poke a few small holes (about an inch apart) at the covered end of the tube. Glue tissue-paper fringe around the end of the horn. Finally, when party time comes, blow your horn while covering the holes with your fingers.

—*Regina John, Queens, New York*

Nifty Noisemakers

These noisemakers are a surefire party-starter. Clean and dry empty water bottles, then fill them with coins, marbles, or beads. Twist the caps back on (tightly!) or glue them shut. Decorate the bottles with glued-on streamers, glitter, or paint. Hand them out to guests when they arrive, and instruct them to shake!

Champagne Pour Technique

Do you love champagne as much as we do? If so, you probably want to avoid over-pouring and spilling the bubbly all over the place. To make sure it all ends up in your glass (and, ultimately, in your mouth), fill only one-third of the glass at a time and wait until the fizz settles before you pour more.

✳ CLASSIC TIP ✳

Champagne lost its fizz? Place a raisin in the glass and the last bits of carbon dioxide that remain will cling to the raisin, then be released again as bubbles. You can also try throwing a few raisins into the bottle before you make the final pour.

Index

who knew?™
online

VISIT OUR WEBSITE AT WhoKnewTips.com!

- Money-saving tips
- Quick 'n' easy recipes
- Who Knew? books and ebooks
- And much more!

Facebook.com/WhoKnewTips
Daily tips, giveaways, and more fun!

Twitter.com/WhoKnewTips
Get a free daily tip and ask us your questions

YouTube.com/WhoKnewTips
Watch demos of your favorite tips

Pinterest.com/WhoKnewTips
Hot tips from around the web!